Th_

20

Best

Bodybuilding
Steroids
On The Market

as well as Growth Hormone and Insulin

Compiled and edited by Robin Barratt

IMPORTANT NOTE:

Not all, but a lot of the information contained herein is the same as in our previous publication *101 Fascinating Facts about Anabolic Steroids in Bodybuilding*. However, For this publication we have added a more detailed introduction, the delivery method for most of the compounds featured, and their current prices on the black market both in the UK and the USA.

LEGAL OR ILLEGAL?

In the UK (as in many other countries) it is **NOT** illegal to possess steroids for one's own use, or to take them. However in the UK it **IS** illegal to sell them, with pretty stiff sentences. However, in the US, Canada and other countries it is illegal to both sell and possess steroids. Some countries you can legally buy steroids over the counter, in other countries you need a prescription. Some countries are very open-minded, others not so much! I have to legally tell you to **ALWAYS** follow the rules and laws of your country with regards to using and possessing steroids.

IS IT OKAY TO USE STEROIDS?

In the UK, in 2014, there were 8,697 alcohol-related deaths. Alcohol is a drug and addictive. Alcohol related harm costs England around £21bn per year, with £3.5bn to the NHS, £11bn tackling alcohol-related crime, and £7.3bn from lost work days and productivity costs. Nicotine is another addictive drug, and is almost guaranteed to kill you in some way. Smoking is the primary cause of preventable illness and premature death, accounting for approximately 100,000 deaths a year in the United Kingdom alone, and at least 600,000 deaths a year globally.

How many people do you think die of steroid use?

It is hard to say as there are no confirmed statistics but maybe... just maybe a handful (and it has been shown that some of these people have had a medical condition anyway, before they started taking steroids). Admittedly, a few more (maybe another handful) people do die of steroid *abuse* (taking huge amounts), but again a tiny, tiny percentage compared to the hundreds of thousands that die each and every year from both smoking and alcohol. And, unlike alcohol and nicotine, steroids are *not* addictive.

Moreover, steroid related harm doesn't cost England a penny either! Steroid related crime? again... virtually nothing! Oh yes, there are no lost working days because of steroid use either!

The media very quickly blames steroid use for the increase aggression and violent behaviour of some bodybuilders and weight-lifters, but have they been into any town on any weekend night; there is violence and aggression everywhere which has nothing to do with steroid use either but everything to do with alcohol use.

There is such a taboo and an excessive and unjustifiable prejudice surrounding steroids and steroid use, and yet the side-effects and dangers and consequences of using steroids are minuscule compared to both alcohol and smoking. And yet smoking and drinking somehow is okay, and accepted, talked about... and even taxed! But taking steroids somehow is not okay, and not accepted and almost never talked about and in some countries, illegal.

Also, why it is legal to sell alcohol and cigarettes which do kill – fact - but illegal to sell steroids? This doesn't make any sense either.

Yes, there are side-effects with taking some steroids (not all) which will be discussed later in this booklet, but there are side-effects with almost every single other drug too, no matter what their use, even Aspirin has side-effects. But, unlike alcohol and smoking, taking steroids almost certainly will not kill you!

Bodybuilders train hard every day. Bodybuilders eat well too; mostly they live pretty healthy lifestyles. Bodybuilders aren't by definition obese or anorexic, most don't smoke or drink either and some (not all) take steroids, but so what?

I remember reading an online survey somewhere asking 100 women that if there was a magic pill they could take every day to keep them younger looking - even if there might be some side effects - would they take it? Guess what? 87 said yes! So what's the difference between bodybuilders taking steroids to help get them in great shape and look good, and a woman taking a pill to keep her younger looking? Pills for keeping young are okay yet pills for getting into shape somehow not okay?

There is, of course, the cheating argument, and the illegal use of steroids in competitive athletics argument too. Firstly let me look briefly at cheating.

How is cheating defined? Is wrinkle cream, face-peels or a stay-young pill for women cheating? Is the development of sports science cheating? Is taking proteins, vitamins, minerals and other sports supplements - all of which are in some way artificially made - cheating? Is having a cup of coffee for caffeine before training cheating? But once again taking a steroid (also artificially made) is unacceptable and defined as cheating. How can taking some supplements be seen as cheating, and others not? How is this 'cheating' defined? By how much, or in what way a certain supplement can help and promote an athlete's performance? Is there a level; a little bit is fine, a lot, not fine?

Which leads us to the steroids in competitive athletics argument. In 2012 Britain achieved their best Olympic gold medal haul in 104 years, eclipsing the 19 they won in Beijing. Almost thirty years ago, in 1980, Britain won just five gold medals! That same year the Soviet Union won 80, and East Germany won 47! Sure, the science of sport has developed considerably over the past few years, but so too has the use of chemicals and synthetic substances in athletics which had significantly enhanced overall performance and ability; the only reason we win more gold medals now is that we have finally caught up with what was once the Soviet-bloc regarding the use of chemicals and doping in competition. If the Soviets didn't use drugs they would have never have won 80 gold medals!

The UK applauds its athletes and the number of golds they win and the records they break and, mostly because of chemicals, they become national heroes... until they get caught of course! If, as recently reported in the media, drug and dope testing is significantly increased over the next few years, our medal count with drop significantly too, and suddenly the UK will once again be ashamed at our athletes' and at our country's poor performance.

It is complete hypocrisy.

Steroids are everywhere, and in EVERY SINGLE sport, whether the public and the media chooses to acknowledge it or not. As an example: just look at the physiques of rugby players now compared to twenty years ago! Without steroids sport will still be at the level it was in the '60s and '70s, before steroids become popular.

I am not advocating or promoting steroid use though; this is your choice alone, not mine!

But if you are going to use steroids, or thinking about using them, and want some quick, easy-to-read basic information in one place, rather than getting lost amongst the thousands of pages and millions of words about steroids on the Internet, and getting confused with the complex structures and explanations, then this is definitely the booklet for you! There are no complicated chemical structures or complex explanations here, just some basic facts and figures, in easy-to-read layman's terms, on the top twenty steroids currently used in bodybuilding today, and how some athletes use them, with current info on the prices they roughly sell for on the black market.

DISCLAIMER

IMPORTANT: The information contained herein is NOT advice, and should NOT be treated as such.

You must not rely on any of the information below as an alternative to advice from an appropriately qualified medical professional and if you think you may be suffering from any adverse medical condition resulting from steroid and related compound use, you should seek immediate medical attention.

The publishers and authors will not be liable in any way in respect of any special, indirect or consequential loss or damage to you because of any of the information contained in this book. **This book is for interest and information purposes only.**

COUNTERFEITS AND FAKES

Most of the steroids on the black market now are counterfeit. Some are fake. What's the difference?

Basically, counterfeit are the real products made by underground manufacturers, fakes are useless and have little or no active compounds, and could actually be very dangerous.

There are lots of underground manufacturers who produce good quality products, at exactly the dosages stated on the labels. There also underground manufacturers that don't, that may label testosterone (for example) as 250mg per ml, but may only contain 150mg per ml. We are not going to list the different manufactured here, as this may be seen as promoting one above the other, plus manufacturers come and go, but if *you are going to buy any steroids, do your research first before you buy!* There is tons of information on the Internet on just about every product and most manufactures, so check them out first, and if the reviews are mixed, stay away. Also, try a small amount first to see if it works and if you see gains. If you don't, don't by that brand again – with social media as it is today, rubbish brands and fake products don't stay around for long and are not as common as they once were fifteen or twenty years ago. Most manufactures realise now that if their products are good, people buy from them again. If they are not, they don't!

MULTI-COMPOUND BLENDS

To make stacking easy, underground labs and manufacturers now produce a huge number of blended products, normally in 10 or 20ml multi-dose vials. A blended product is two or more compounds in one dose. The compounds used in blends tend to be the ones that work most effectively together.

Just a very few examples;

TriTest 500 (200mg Testosterone Cypionate, 200mg Testosterone Deconate, 100mg Testosterone Enanthate).

DecaTest 500 (200mg Deca-Durabolin, 200mg Testosterone Decanoate, 100mg Testosterone Cypionate).

Nandrotest 200 (67mg Nandrolone Phenyl Propionate, 133mg Testosterone Propionate).

Equitest 800 (400mg Boldenone Undecylenate, 400mg Testosterone Decanoate).

Equitren 800 (500mg Boldenone Undecylenate, 300mg Trenbolone Enanthate).

Eqtrenmast 800 (300mg Boldenone Undecylenate, 250mg Trenbolone Enanthate, 250mg Drostanolone Enanthate).

TrenProp 200 (75mg Trenbolone Acetate, 125mg Testosterone Propionate).

TrenOxyProp 200 (50mg Trenbolone Acetate, 50mg Oxymethelone, 100mg Testosterone Propionate).

TNTMAST 250 (75mg Trenbolone Acetate, 100mg Testosterone Propionate, 75mg Masterone Propionate).

TNTMAST 400 (100mg Trenbolone Enanthate, 200mg Testosterone Cypionate, 100mg Masterone Enanthate).

Trenrip 300 (150mg Tren Acetate, 75mg Testosterone Propionate, 75mg Masterone Propionate).

SIDE EFFECTS

Different steroids have different side-effects, and various levels of side effects. Plus, of course, everyone's anatomy and physiology is different too, so one person might be affected much more, or much less, than someone else using the same compound in the same amounts. If you decide to take steroids, always seek medical advice if you are unsure of how the compound is affecting you, or if you experience severe side-effects.

These can be some of the major side-effects associated with steroid use, more specifics are detailed in each compound featured:

Gynocomastia is the development of the breast tissue in males due to an excess of estrogen present in the body a result of aromatization where androgens, for example testosterone are converted to estrogen. This happens as the estrogen binds itself to the receptors in the breast tissue. Noticed at first by an itchiness of the nipples, followed by pain, and swelling. The two most common ways to counteract gynecomastia are the use an anti-estrogen compounds like Nolvadex, Anastrozole or Clomiphene Citrate or a Aromatase Inhibitor like Aromastab or Letrozole.

Inhibition of natural hormones is the most common side effect bodybuilders have by using anabolic steroids and hormones. To keep a natural balance in the body, taking synthetic hormones will send a message to your body's system to reduce or stop producing its own. Depending upon the steroids and hormones used, the body either shuts down completely or reduces mildly. In order to counter this, bodybuilders use Human Chorionic Gonadotropin, anti-estrogens and Estrogen blockers. The effects that steroids and hormones have on the body's system are almost always reversible on cessation of steroid and hormone therapy.

Liver damage. Most oral steroids pass through he liver; the body´s filtration system. Most medical research on steroids focus on the fact that, following ingestion, liver enzymes are elevated but in most cases research has also shown that this doesn't necessarily mean liver damage, only with the most abused compounds. Research has also shown that liver enzymes almost always return to normal from between three months and one year after steroid use, depending upon the compounds used and the dosages.

Effects on cholesterol levels. Steroids can lower HDL (good cholesterol) levels - which helps to protect the arteries by bringing unused cholesterol to the liver where it is broken down - and raise LDL cholesterol - which can build up on the inside of artery walls, contributing to artery blockages that can lead to heart attacks. Research has shown, however, that levels return to normal fairly soon after steroid discontinuation.

Acne. Bodybuilders very often experience bouts of acne whilst on steroids, the severity of which depends upon the types of steroids used and the dosages. High androgenic steroids can increase sebaceous gland activity which promotes oily skin which then combines with bacteria to clog pores.

Steroid Rage. High androgenic steroids can sometimes increase aggressiveness in some users, especially those with naturally aggressive tendencies and, in some rare cases, significant psychiatric changes can occur including raised aggression levels, and an increased disposition to violence, mania, and even psychosis. There are many bodybuilders however that never experience any change in behaviour or emotional state while on steroids, which means general temperament clearly plays a large role in how a bodybuilder responds psychologically to steroid administration.

Hair loss. Steroids can cause men to start balding if they have a genetic predisposition towards Male Pattern Baldness, because the scalp strongly reacts to Dihydrotestosterone, which many steroids convert to, or are derived from. Anti hair-loss medications such as Finasteride and Dutesteride can help prevent this.

Cardiovascular Problems. Research has shown that anabolic steroids have been linked with cardiovascular issues due to their effects on blood lipids. Many bodybuilders however have been found to have enlarged ventricles due to the nature of their sport and the stress it has on their heart, rather than solely on steroid use.

Water Retention and Bloating. Water retention is a fairly common side effect with specific androgenic steroids including the testosterones, especially when on bulking cycles. This can normally be countered by using anti-estrogenic compounds like Nolvadex. Also bodybuilders use diuretics to help rid fluids from the body. Sodium, sugar, and synthetic sweeteners can also contribute to bloating and water retention so cutting these out helps too.

Sterility. Temporary sterility is a very common side effect of steroids and hormones in both males and females. In fact small dosages of testosterone have been studied and approved by the World Health Organization as a possibility for male contraception. For women steroids disrupt the hormones that regulates regular menstrual cycles, and for men steroids lower Follicle Stimulating Hormone (FSH) to the point where normal production of sperm is not possible. Sterility is temporary though and reverses post-cycle.

LASTLY...

Every well-muscled film and TV star, fitness presenter, singer and celebrity most likely takes steroids to help them look the way they do - just look at how the physiques of Dwayne Johnson, Mark Wahlberg, Vin Diesel, Chris Hemsworth (to name just four!) have changed over the years. This isn't done with milk and egg powder! Anabolic steroids are the new designer drug of the 21st Century, with virtually all of the well developed physiques on stage and screen built on a combination of steroids and Growth Hormones. Fact.

AN INTRODUCTION TO STEROIDS

Anabolic steroids were first made commercially in the 1930s to treat chronic wasting conditions, and then used significantly during the Second World War to stimulate muscle growth for burns victims and severe muscular injury.

During the 1940s and '50s, experiments with steroids continued and their use widened among athletes and bodybuilders, especially in the Soviet Union and Eastern Bloc countries. The overwhelming domination by these countries in weightlifting events at the 1952 Olympics, prompted U.S. Olympic Team physician Dr. John Ziegler to begin issuing steroids to his athletes. Heavy use of steroids and hormones became widespread in bodybuilding in the early '60s. The use of Human Growth Hormone, both on its own and in conjunction with insulin and IGF1 injections, and stacked with steroids and hormones and Post Cycle Therapy (PCT) compounds, became widespread in the sport of bodybuilding in the mid '90s.

Bodybuilders use two main types of steroids; anabolic androgenic steroids (AAS) and androgenic hormones (AH). Although both have androgenic and anabolic properties, they both work in very different ways.

Muscle mass induced by androgens mainly arise from cellular enlargement rather than cellular proliferation, whereas muscle mass induced by anabolics mainly arise from cellular proliferation rather than cellular enlargement. Cellular enlargement is what is says, the enlargement of individual cells. Cellular proliferation is an increase in the number of cells. Hence bodybuilders use both anabolics and androgens for maximum gains. The word 'mainly' is used as both androgens and anabolics actually do both proliferation and enlargement and to varying degrees.

Androgenic hormones or androgens, is the broad term for any natural or synthetic compound that stimulates or controls the development and maintenance of male characteristics which, specifically for bodybuilders, includes muscle mass, strength, and aggression (for intensive training). The primary and most well-known androgen is testosterone.

Anabolic steroids is the broad term for any natural or synthetic compound that increases protein synthesis in the body. The fuel that the body needs to build muscle tissue is protein. If bodybuilders don't get enough protein they simply won't be able to build maximum muscle. Bodybuilders using anabolic steroids need to consume between at least 1g and 1.5g of protein per pound of bodyweight every day. The American College of Sports Medicine acknowledges that anabolic steroids, in the presence of adequate diet, can contribute to a significant increases in body-weight, often as lean muscle mass increases, and gains in muscular strength and endurance achieved through high-intensity exercise and proper diet.

Virtually all anabolic steroids have various degrees of androgenic properties too, which includes the development and maintenance of masculine characteristics. The ratio of anabolic and androgenic properties depends upon the specific compound and therefore its particular and specific use in bodybuilding.

Bodybuilders take steroids orally and by injection. Some steroids are commercially available transdermally, but these compounds are not in any strong enough doses for effective use by bodybuilders.

An anabolic steroid cycle simply refers to the period of actual steroid use; when steroids are being administered, this is often referred to as an On-Cycle.

When they are not it is commonly known as an Off-Cycle.

Steroid stacks refer to the combination of anabolic steroids being used during a steroid cycle, as well as the non-steroidal items that may also be included during this phase including Post Cycle Therapy (PCT).

For the average bodybuilder, steroid cycles normally last between 8 and 22 weeks, with between 4 and 12 weeks off (clean). However, many top professional and competitive bodybuilders never come off steroids and / or Post Cycle Therapy, but move to different stacks and cycles throughout the year and according to their training and competitive schedule. When choosing steroids stacks, bodybuilders choose the appropriate combinations of compounds depending upon their goals at a time, whether bulking, cutting or enhancing athletic performance. As these goals change, so do the types of steroids used.

Milligram for milligram, there is no anabolic steroid better than testosterone in terms of all-purpose and all-round use. The more Testosterone you take, the bigger and stronger you become, it really is as simple as that. Testosterone is the perfect instrument for building muscle and increasing strength, as well as in the preservation of both muscle mass and strength. Testosterone is used for bulking, cutting and / or for athletic endurance, and is what all other anabolic steroids ratios are measured against. Testosterones anabolic / androgenic ratio is 1:1 meaning it is exactly as anabolic as it is androgenic. If a steroid is 2:1, then it is, compared with testosterones ratio, doubly as anabolic as it is androgenic.

Healthy young adult men produce between 3mg and 10mg of testosterone per day. Starting at approximately 40 years of age, testosterone levels drop by approximately 10% every decade in men. Bodybuilders can and often take between 250mg and 2000mg of testosterone a week, that's from between

3 and 300 times what the body naturally produces.

THE 20 BEST STEROIDS ON THE MARKET

(in no particular ratings order)

NOTE: items are listed in compound name with the most common brand or product name in brackets.

1. **Testosterone Cypionate**
2. **Testosterone Enanthate**
3. **Testosterone Propionate**
4. **Testosterone Heptylate**
5. **Testosterone Decanoate**
6. **Testosterone Unecanoate**
7. **Methyl-testosterone**
8. **Fluoxymesterone (Halotestin)**
9. **Oxymetholone (Anapolon 50)**
10. **Trenbolone Acetate (Parabolon)**
11. **Nandrolone Decanoate (Deca Durabolin)**
12. **Methandrostenolone (Dianabol)**
13. **Boldenone Undecylenate (Equipoise)**
14. **Methenolone Enanthate (Primobolan)**
15. **Oxandrolone (Anavar)**
16. **Stanozolol (Winstrol)**
17. **Drostanolone Enanthate (Masteron)**
18. **Mesterolone (Proviron)**
19. **Stenbolone (Anatrofin)**
20. **Sanabolicum**

plus.... **Growth Hormone and Insulin**

Notes on prices. *Prices throughout the book are based on the black market in both the UK and the US at the time of writing this booklet (May 2016). However, because steroids are illegal to posses in the USA, costs are significantly more than in the UK where steroids are not illegal to posses.*

TESTOSTERONE CYPIONATE

Testosterone Cypionate is an injectable hormone with a tremendous metabolic enhancer used by bodybuilders to increase mass, strength, conditioning, as well as promoting recovery and rejuvenation.

Testosterone is a hormone produced by all human-beings and is the primary male sex hormone. This hormone is responsible for the many different physical and mental characteristics in males including; sex drive, fat loss, gaining and maintaining lean muscle mass, deepening of the voice and increases bone density. These traits do not change, whether testosterone is produced naturally or synthetically.

Testosterone promotes nitrogen retention in the muscle and the more nitrogen the muscles hold the more protein the muscles store. Testosterone also increases levels of IGF-1 providing even more anabolic activity and muscle growth, and has the ability to increase the activity of satellite cells which play an active role in repairing damaged muscle tissue.

Testosterone is the *father* of all anabolic steroids used by bodybuilders today and all testosterone compounds carry an anabolic / androgenic score of 100; a rating used to measure all other steroids by. Testosterones promotes massive muscle gains and is dosage dependent - the higher the dose the higher the muscle building effect. As well as off-season mass and muscle building, Testosterone Cypionate can be hugely beneficial during the cutting and dieting phase too, as it preserves lean muscle tissue that could otherwise be lost with a restricted diet and intense training and cardio.

To keep blood levels peaked, bodybuilders have found

it more effective to take two smaller injections a week, rather than just one larger dose once a week. Dosages can range anywhere from 250mg to 2000mg per week, depending on needs and goals and contest preparation schedule.

Testosterone Cypionate can be used for long periods, with 16 to 22 week cycles not uncommon, however, many bodybuilders never come off testosterone but Post Cycle Therapy (PCT) will be needed for those bodybuilders coming off testosterone after an extended period.

As with almost all testosterone compounds, Testosterone Cypionate carries a high level of aromatase activity, which can lead to gynecomastia and excess water retention, as well as other androgen related side effects including acne, hair loss and prostate enlargement.

Testosterone Cypionate for women is not recommended.

The active life of the compound is 8 days and it can be detected in the system for up to 3 months.

DELIVERY

Cypionate is generally produced in a strength of either 200mg per 1ml, or 250mg per 1ml. It is possible to buy 1ml ampoules of Cypionate, however most manufacturers sell Cypionate in either 10ml or 20ml vials.

COSTS

Approximate costs of Testosterone Cypionate on the black market (in GBP / USD) at the time of writing this booklet (May 2016):

- 1ml x 250mg single dose ampoule 5 GBP / 10 USD

- 10ml x 250mg per ml multi-dose vial between 30 and 40 GBP / 60 and 80 USD.
- 20ml x 250mg per ml multi-dose vial between 40 and 50 GBP / 80 and 100 USD.

TESTOSTERONE ENANTHATE

Testosterone Enanthate is an injectable hormone with a tremendous metabolic enhancer used by bodybuilders to increase mass, strength, conditioning, as well as promoting recovery and rejuvenation. It can also help with losing fat. Testosterone Enanthate is probably the most commonly used form of testosterone by bodybuilders worldwide.

As with Testosterone Cypionate, Testosterone Enanthate promotes nitrogen retention in the muscle and the more nitrogen the muscles hold the more protein the muscles store. Testosterone Enanthate also increases levels of IGF-1 providing even more anabolic activity and muscle growth, and has the ability to increase the activity of satellite cells which play an active role in repairing damaged muscle tissue.

To keep blood levels peaked, like Cypionate above, bodybuilders have found it more effective to take one smaller injections of Enanthate every five days, rather than just one larger dose every ten days.

As with Cypionate, Testosterone Enanthate can also be used for long periods, with 16 to 22 week cycles not uncommon, however, many bodybuilders never come off testosterone but Post Cycle Therapy (PCT) will be needed for those bodybuilders coming off testosterone after an extended period.

As with almost all testosterone compounds, Testosterone Enanthate carries a high level of aromatase activity, which can lead to gynecomastia and excess water retention, as well as other androgen related side effects including acne, hair loss and prostate enlargement.

Testosterone Enanthate for women is not

recommended.

Male bodybuilders take between 500 to 2000mg a week. Enanthate has all the same properties as Testosterone Cypionate (above), it's active life is 10.5 days and can be detected in the system for up to 3 months.

DELIVERY

Testosterone Enanthate is generally produced in a strength of either 200mg per 1ml, or 250mg per 1ml. It is possible to buy 1ml ampoules of Enanthate, however most manufacturers sell Enanthate in either 10ml or 20ml vials.

COSTS

Approximate costs of Testosterone Enanthate on the black market (in GBP / USD) at the time of writing this booklet (May 2016):

- 1ml x 250mg single dose ampoule 5 GBP / 10 USD
- 10ml x 250mg per ml multi-dose vial between 30 and 40 GBP / 60 and 80 USD.
- 20ml x 250mg per ml multi-dose vial between 40 and 50 GBP / 80 and 100 USD.

TESTOSTERONE PROPIONATE

Testosterone Propionate is an injectable hormone used by bodybuilders to increase mass, strength, conditioning, as well as promoting recovery and rejuvenation and has virtually the same properties as the other two testosterones above, aside from Propionate is faster acting; is has an active life of just 2 to 3 days, which means, for maximum effect, injections should be administered every 2 to 3 days.

Testosterone Propionate is also a relatively safe steroid to use, with some studies showing no adverse effects from a 20 week cycle at 600mgs a week. Testosterone Propionate causes the least side effects than the other testosterones, and the least water retention, and is often the testosterone of choice in cutting cycles. For more rapid gains, Testosterone Propionate is frequently used by bodybuilders as a front-loading compound, where much larger dosages are injected over the first two weeks of a cycle, in conjunction with longer acting testosterones, in order to raise the blood levels of the hormone quickly and until the longer-acting testosterone kicks in, and then the Propionate stopped.

Testosterone Propionate stacks well with almost every other steroid. Although fast-acting, it can still be detected in the system for up to 3 weeks.

Male bodybuilders take between 300mg to 2000mg a week, with females taking between 50 and 100mgs a week.

DELIVERY

Testosterone Propionate is generally produced in a strength of 100mg per 1ml. It is also available from some manufacturers at 200mg per 1ml, however at this dosage if not mixed with Ethyl Oleate, the injection site can often be extremely painful and take quite a while to dissipate. It is possible to buy 1ml ampoules of Propionate, however most manufacturers sell Propionate in either 10ml or 20ml vials.

COSTS

Approximate costs of Testosterone Propionate on the black market (in GBP / USD) at the time of writing this booklet (May 2016):

- 1ml x 100mg single dose ampoule 4 GBP / 8 USD
- 10ml x 100mg per ml multi-dose vial between 30 and 40 GBP / 60 and 80 USD.
- 20ml x 100mg per ml multi-dose vial between 40 and 50 GBP / 80 and 100 USD.
- 20ml x 200mg per ml multi-dose vial between 50 and 60 GBP / 100 and 120 USD.

TESTOSTERONE HEPTYLATE

Testosterone Heptylate is a long-acting injectable testosterone used by many bodybuilders for the rapid build-up of strength and muscle mass.

Many bodybuilders report that, milligram for milligram Testosterone Heptylate has a stronger effect than Testosterone Enanthate, Cypionate and Propionate. Also, Testosterone Heptylate promotes a high degree of recovery and, after only just a couple of days of starting the compound, bodybuilders report an tremendous pump during the workout and a noticeable increase in appetite.

Side effects are comparable to the other testosterones mentioned above, but when water retention does occur it is usually lower than with Enantathe and Cypionate. Some studies showing no adverse effects from a 20 week cycle at 500mgs a week.

Testosterone Heptylate has an active life of up to 20 days and can be detected in the system up to 3 months. Most bodybuilders inject at least once a week, with an average dose of between 250mg and 1000mg a week, while women use between 50mg to 100mg a week.

DELIVERY

Testosterone Heptylate is generally produced in a strength of 200mg per 1ml. It is also available from some manufacturers at 300mg per 1ml. It is possible to buy 1ml ampoules of Heptylate at both 200mg and 300mg per ml, however most manufacturers sell Heptylate in 10ml vials.

COSTS

Approximate costs of Testosterone Heptylate on the black market (in GBP / USD) at the time of writing this booklet (May 2016):

- 1ml x 200mg single dose ampoule 5 GBP / 10 USD
- 1ml x 300mg single dose ampoule 6 GBP / 12 USD
- 10ml x 200mg per ml multi-dose vial between 30 and 40 GBP / 60 and 80 USD.
- 10ml x 300mg per ml multi-dose vial between 40 and 50 GBP / 80 and 100 USD.

TESTOSTERONE DECANOATE

Like all the above testosterones, **Testosterone Decanoate** is used by bodybuilders for the build-up of strength and quality muscle, and is probably most known as being a compound of the testosterone blend Sustanon 250.

Side effects are comparable to the other testosterones mentioned above. Some studies showing no adverse effects from a 20 week cycle at 500mgs a week.

Decanoate has an active life of up to 15 days and can be detected in the system up to 3 months. Most bodybuilders inject at least once a week, with an average dose of between 250mg and 2000mg a week, although 500mg per week has produced excellent results with many bodybuilders.

Testosterone Decanoate for women is not recommended.

DELIVERY

Testosterone Decanoate is generally produced in a strength of 100mg, 200mg and 250mg per 1ml in either 10ml or 20ml multi-dose vials There are also 1 x 4ml single-dose ampoules x 1000mg, and 1 x 2ml single-dose ampoules x 200mg available.

COSTS

Approximate costs of Testosterone Decanoate on the black market (in GBP / USD) at the time of writing this booklet (May 2016):

- 4ml x 1000mg single dose ampoule 25 GBP / 50 USD
- 2ml x 200mg single dose ampoule 6 GBP / 12

USD
- 10ml x 200mg per ml multi-dose vial between 30 and 40 GBP / 60 and 80 USD.
- 20ml x 200mg per ml multi-dose vial between 40 and 50 GBP / 80 and 100 USD.

TESTOSTERONE UNDECANOATE

Testosterone Undecanoate is an oral testosterone used by bodybuilders for the more slower build-up of strength and quality muscle and conditioning, and as an alternative to methyl-testosterone which can be harsh on the liver.

Oral Testosterone Undecanoate is dissolved in caster oil and propelyne glycol laurate, which makes the compound fat-soluble and therefore able to be absorbed through the small intestine via the lymphatic system. This means that the first-pass through the liver is avoided, which could destroy much of the active steroid, as well as place unwanted stress on the liver.

Oral Testosterone Undecanoate does not affect blood pressure, has no adverse effects on the prostate and fewer estrogenic side-effects. However, because this product peaks testosterone levels in about two hours and has an active life of between 8 and 12 hours, is not only awkward to take - bodybuilders need to take at least two capsules of 40mg every two to three hours continuously for any significant anabolic effects to be seen - but can work out extremely expensive compared to traditional testosterones. But this is definitely the choice for many older bodybuilders wanting smaller gains with a safer oral testosterone compound and for those bodybuilders not wanting to inject.

Testosterone Undecanoate for women is not recommended.

DELIVERY

Testosterone Undecanoate capsules are generally produced in a strength of 40mg per capsule. We have also just recently noticed one manufacturer producing an injectable form of Testosterone Undecanoate at a strength of 1000mg per 4 ml single dose ampoule.

COSTS

Approximate costs of Testosterone Undecanoate on the black market (in GBP / USD) at the time of writing this booklet (May 2016):

- 30 x 40mg capsules 40 GBP / 80 USD
- 1 x 4ml x 1000mg single dose ampoule between 25 and 35 GBP / 50 and 70 USD

METHYL-TESTOSTERONE

Methyl-testosterone is an oral testosterone used by bodybuilders for the build-up of strength and quality muscle and conditioning and also by power-lifters and other strength athletes prior to competition as, like all testosterones, aggression can be significantly increased.

Methyl-testosterone can take approximately two hours for levels to peak in the body, so it is used by bodybuilders to elevate their testosterone levels very quickly and, like Propionate, often used for the first week or two in order to raise the blood levels of the hormone quickly and until longer-acting testosterone kicks in, and then the Methyl-testosterone stopped.

Methyl-testosterone is an oral testosterone hormone and one of the oldest anabolic steroids in existence and, because testosterone was the first anabolic steroid ever synthesized, one of the most important steroids ever created.

The side effects of Methyl-testosterone can be more pronounced and significant than most other testosterone compounds and can include: acne, accelerated hair loss, body hair growth, high blood pressure, water retention and loss / increase in libido.

Bodybuilders who do take Methyl-testosterone normally take around 50mg a day for a couple of weeks at the beginning of a cycle, or for 6 to 8 week as part of a cycle.

It is not suitable for women. It has an active life of 6 to 8 hours, so dosages should be split up. It can be detected in the body for up to six weeks.

Methyl-testosterone for women is not recommended.

DELIVERY

Methyl-testosterone capsules are almost always produced in a strength of 25mg per capsule.

COSTS

Approximate costs of Methyl-testosterone on the black market (in GBP / USD) at the time of writing this booklet (May 2016):

- 50 x 25mg capsules between 25 and 35 GBP / 50 and 70 USD

FLUOXYMESTERONE

Fluoxymesterone, commonly known as Halotestin, is a legendary oral steroid which will increase strength more dramatically than any other steroid. Mainly used by athletics, strength athletes and power-lifters, however bodybuilders often use it in the final weeks before a contest to harden up an already lean physique and give some added aggression during the final workouts before a contest.

Fluoxymesterone has no estrogenic activity and so won't cause water retention or the other side-effects associated with estrogen, however it is fairly liver-toxic.

Fluoxymesterone also has a volumising effect on the physique which, for bodybuilders with a low body-fat percentage, will cause an immediately contest ready fuller appearance.

Fluoxymesterone has an active life of 6 to 8 hours and bodybuilders normally take around 40mg per day, divided up, for a maximum of 4 to 6 weeks and can be detected in the system for up to 2 months.

Fluoxymesterone is unsuitable for women.

DELIVERY

Fluoxymesterone capsules are almost always produced in a strength of 10mg per tablet.

COSTS

Approximate costs of Fluoxymesterone on the black market (in GBP / USD) at the time of writing this booklet (May 2016):

- 50 x 10mg tablets between 40 and 50 GBP /

80 and 100 USD

OXYMETHOLONE

Oxymetholone commonly known as Anapolon 50, is a extremely potent oral steroid developed in 1960 by Zoltan and used by bodybuilders for massive mass, size and strength gains. Bodybuilders who are following a good bulking diet high in protein, can expect increases of 20lbs (10kg) in weight in a matter of just a few weeks, with even higher weight increases commonly reported.

Oxymetholone is highly hepatotoxic (liver-toxic) and long-term use of the drug can cause a variety of serious side-effects including hepatitis, cirrhosis and liver cancer, and therefore most bodybuilders never take Oxymetholone for any longer than 4 to 6 weeks.

Many competitive bodybuilders also successfully use Oxymetholone to give the physique a fuller look in the final weeks of their contest preparation, as the steroid responds well to carbohydrates, which many bodybuilders ingested during this phase.

Common side-effects are pronounced water retention, high blood-pressure, gynecomastia and acne. As with most steroids, Oxymetholone also suppress natural testosterone so it is important to use a testosterone compound alongside it. The average dose is 50mg to 100mg a day.

Oxymetholone is not suitable for women.

DELIVERY

Oxymetholone tablets are almost always produced in a strength of 50mg per tablet.

COSTS

Approximate costs of Oxymetholone on the black

market (in GBP / USD) at the time of writing this booklet (May 2016):

- 50 x 50mg tablets between 40 - 60 GBP / 80 – 120 USD

TRENBOLONE ACETATE

Trenbolone Acetate is an powerful injectable steroid considered by many bodybuilders to be one of the greatest anabolic steroids on the market today.

It has an extreme metabolic enhancer and is used for all purposes; it is one of the best bulking steroids available promoting size and strength available, and its tremendous cutting and conditioning properties are unrivalled. In fact, you could stack numerous other anabolic steroids together and still not reach the level of power in Trenbolone. Also, during the cutting phase, there is no anabolic steroid on the market today that is as beneficial, as powerful, or as valuable as Trenbolone.

Trenbolone was originally manufactured by Negma Laboratories, France, under the name Parabolan, but was discontinued in 1997. Trenbolone is simply a modified form of the Nandrolone hormone which puts it in the same category as Deca-Durabolin but, because of its tremendous benefits to bodybuilders, Trenbolone is perhaps the most sought after injectable steroid on the market.

It has an active half-life from 48 to slightly less than 72 hours and is a fairly fast-acting steroid so injections should take place frequently in order to maintain stable blood levels.

Trenbolone will greatly enhance protein synthesis and nitrogen retention in the muscle tissue, requiring an appropriate amount of protein to be consumed for maximum beneficial effect. Trenbolone does not aromatize at all, which is the very reason excess water retention is impossible with this steroid. However, like any other highly androgenic hormone, side-effects include gynecomastia, acne, accelerated hair loss, in fact Trenbolone can be one of the unfriendliest steroids for hair loss. It can also have a strong, negative impact on cholesterol, so a cholesterol-friendly diet is imperative. Also, Trenbolone significantly suppresses the body's natural testosterone level and in extremely high doses can cause anxiety, insomnia, night-sweats, and rapid heart rate.

Although some bodybuilders take up to 200mg every other day, for most bodybuilders, 100mg every other day seems to produce the best results.

Trenbolone is unsuitable for women.

DELIVERY

Trenbolone is generally produced in a strength of 100mg, 150mg and 200mgper ml, in 10ml and 20ml multi-dose vials, as well as 76mg per ml in a 1.5 ml singe dose ampoule.

COSTS

Approximate costs of Trenbolone on the black market (in GBP / USD) at the time of writing this booklet (May 2016):

- 1.5ml x 76mg/ml single dose ampoule between 7 and 10 GBP / 14 and 20 USD.
- 10ml x 100mg per ml multi-dose vial, between 45 and 55 GBP / 90 and 100 USD
- 10ml x 200mg per ml multi-dose vial, between 50 and 60 GBP / 100 and 120 USD
- 20ml x 100mg per ml multi-dose vial, between 55 and 65 GBP / 110 and 130 USD
- 20ml x 200mg per ml multi-dose vial, between 70 and 80 GBP / 140 and 160 USD

NANDROLONE DECANOATE

Nandrolone Decanoate is an injectable steroid commonly used by bodybuilders to promote size, mass and tissue growth. It also strongly promotes joint relief. More commonly known as Deca, Nandrolone Decanoate is one of the most widely used injectable steroids on the market, and one of the very first ever steroids used by professional bodybuilders.

It has an active life of 15 days with a slow release Nandrolone Decanoate can be detectable in a drug screen for up to 18 months, Nandrolone Decanoate has also been detected in more competitive athletes than almost any other steroid.

Liver toxicity is low but effects such as gynaecomastia and reduced libido still occur in large doses. Other side-effect of very high levels Nandrolone Decanoate use can include erectile dysfunction and cardiovascular damage.

In a bulking cycle bodybuilders usually use up to 600mg a week over a 12 to 16 week period, or 200mg to 400mg in a cutting cycle, as long as something to combat water retention is present. Women tend to use between 50mg to 100mg a week for both bulking and cutting.

DELIVERY

Nandrolone Decanoate is generally produced in a strength of 250mg per 1ml in either 10ml or 20ml multi-dose vials There are also 1 x 1ml x 250mg single-dose ampoules , 1 x 2ml x 250mg single-dose ampoules, and 1 x 2ml x 200mg single-dose ampoules available.

COSTS

Approximate costs of Nandrolone Decanoate on the black market (in GBP / USD) at the time of writing this booklet (May 2016):

- 1ml x 250mg single dose ampoule between 5 and 6 GBP / 10 and 12 USD.
- 2ml x 200mg single dose ampoule between 5 and 6 GBP / 10 and 12 USD.
- 10ml x 250mg per ml multi-dose vial between 40 and 50 GBP / 80 and 100 USD.
- 20ml x 250mg per ml multi-dose vial between 40 and 60 GBP / 80 and 120 USD

METHANDROSTENOLONE

Methandrostenolone, more commonly known as Dianabol, is one of the first oral anabolic steroids ever created for the purpose of performance enhancement, and the most widely used today. Most bodybuilders will say extremely hard to beat and one of the very best anabolic steroids used by bodybuilders to promote mass, size, strength and muscular endurance.

The active life of oral Methandrostenolone is 6 to 8 hours with a half-life of only about 3 to 5 hours which means that a single daily dosage will produce unwanted ups and downs in blood levels throughout the day so bodybuilders usually divide their dosage up throughout the day in order to regulate the concentration of the compound in the body.

Side effects common with Dianabol include oily skin, acne, body and facial hair growth, male pattern baldness and increased aggression, and because it does aromatize, can cause a lot of water retention.

Daily dosages range from 25mg to 50mg, although some bodybuilders do take up to 100mg a day. Because results can be seen within a week, many bodybuilders use Dianabol in the first 3 to 6 weeks of their cycle and until their injectables start to kick in, and then they come off the compound. It is not advisable to stay on Dianabol for longer than 6 weeks.

DELIVERY

Methandrostenolone is generally produced in a strength of 5mg and 10mg per tablet. Note, recently there has been an injectable version of Methandrostenolone available from more specialised manufacturers at a dosage of 25mg per ml.

COSTS

Approximate costs of Methandrostenolone on the black market (in GBP / USD) at the time of writing this booklet (May 2016):

- 100 x 5mg tablets between 15 and 20 GBP / 30 and 40 USD
- 100 x 10mg tablets between 25 and 35 GBP / 50 and 70 USD
- 500 x 10mg tablets between 80 and 100 GBP / 160 and 200 USD
- 10ml x 25mg per ml multi-dose vial between 25 and 35 GBP / 50 and 70 USD

BOLDENONE UNDECYLENATE

Boldenone Undecylenate, more commonly known as Equipoise is an injectable steroid used by bodybuilders to promote strength, recovery and conditioning, and mass if used alongside other bulking compounds.

Although Equipoise was originally created by scientists attempting to make a long acting injectable Dianabol, the final product is very different. Equipoise is just as anabolic as the Testosterones, but only half as androgenic, which means bodybuilders can't gain the same amount of weight as they could with an equal amount of Testosterone. However, athletes almost never report estrogenic side-effects with Equipoise, even when the dose is up to 1 gram per week.

Most bodybuilders take between 200mg to 800mg a week, and for women from between 50mg to 100mg a week.

Because it is a long-acting compound with an active life of 15 days, cycles should be for no less than 12 weeks. Equipoise can also detectable in drug tests for up to 6 months after finishing the cycle.

DELIVERY

Boldenone Undecylenate is generally produced in a strength of 250mg and 500mg per ml, in 1 ml single dose ampoules and 10ml and 20ml multi-dose vials.

COSTS

Approximate costs of Boldenone Undecylenate on the black market (in GBP / USD) at the time of writing this booklet (May 2016):

- 1ml x 250mg single dose ampoule between 5 and 6 GBP / 10 and 12 USD.
- 10ml x 250mg per ml multi-dose vial, between 30 and 40 GBP / 60 and 80 USD
- 20ml x 250mg per ml multi-dose vial, between 50 and 60 GBP / 100 and 120 USD
- 20ml x 500mg per ml multi-dose vial, between 75 and 90 GBP / 150 and 180 USD

METHENOLONE ENANTHATE

Methenolone Enanthate, more commonly known as Primobolan Depot, or Primo, is an injectable steroid used by bodybuilders for conditioning, recovery and rejuvenation, as well as to help preserve muscle tissue during cutting phase.

Methenolone can also be used for mass building alongside mass-building compounds.

Methenolone is not converted into estrogen so there are fewer side-effects than many other compounds, however, due to the androgenic residual effect, some side-effects might include acne, deepening of the voice and / or increased hair growth and, at higher dosages, some water retention can sometimes occur.

Methenolone is generally one of the safest injectable steroids bodybuilders use. The normal dose bodybuilders take is between 200 to 600 mg per week, depending upon what other compounds are being used at the same time.

Women normally prefer the 25mg tablets, but there are female bodybuilders who inject between 100mg to 200mg of Methenolone Enanthate a week.

DELIVERY

Methenolone is generally produced in a strength of 100mg per ml, in 1 ml single dose ampoules and 10ml and 20ml multi-dose vials, as well as 25mg tablets.

COSTS

Approximate costs of Methenolone on the black market (in GBP / USD) at the time of writing this booklet (May 2016):

- 50 x 25mg tablets between 35 and 45 GBP / 70 and 90 USD
- 1ml x 100mg single dose ampoule between 5 and 6 GBP / 10 and 12 USD.
- 10ml x 100mg per ml multi-dose vial, between 50 and 60 GBP / 100 and 120 USD
- 20ml x 100mg per ml multi-dose vial, between 70 and 80 GBP / 140 and 160 USD

OXANDROLONE

Oxandrolone, more commonly known as Anavar, is a fairly safe oral steroid great for moderate strength gains as well as for cutting and conditioning. Gains from Oxandrolone are solid with a large percentage retained post-usage.

Because it is an extremely mild steroid, much larger dosages are needed for any significant results, with most male bodybuilders using between 80mg and 100mg a day and, between 10mg and 20mg a day for female bodybuilders, with 12 to 16 week cycles are fairly usual.

Many bodybuilders use Oxandrolone prior to contest for its fat burning properties and, in one study, abdominal and trunk fat was significantly reduced on dosages as little as 20mg a day. Many bodybuilders use Oxandrolone in between their cycles too, as an active fat-burner and to retain previous made gains with other compounds.

The active life is between 8 and 12 hours, so dosages are best split up to 2 or 3 times a day, and the detection time in the body is around 3 weeks.

Most side effects often found with other steroids are not found with Oxandrolone and so it is often the steroid of choice for many female bodybuilders.

DELIVERY

Oxandrolone is generally produced in a strength of 10mg, 20mg and 50mg tablets.

COSTS

Approximate costs of Oxandrolone on the black market (in GBP / USD) at the time of writing this booklet (May 2016):

- 50 x 10mg tablets between 35 and 45 GBP / 70 and 90 USD
- 50 x 20mg tablets between 60 and 70 GBP / 120 and 140 USD
- 50 x 50mg tablets between 60 and 75 GBP / 120 and 150 USD

STANOZOLOL

Stanozolol, more commonly known as Winstrol, or Winni, is both an injectable and oral steroid almost always used by bodybuilders for cutting and conditioning.

It has strong metabolic enhancing properties and greatly improves muscular endurance, which is why it is one of the most widely used steroids across the athletic field in general.

The injectable version of Stanozolol is much more effective and popular than the tablets.

Unusually, Stanozolol is dissolved in water and not oil, which means it has a relatively low half-life and so, for best results, bodybuilders inject daily or every second day.

Alongside a low calorie, protein-rich diet, Stanozolol gives muscles a much harder appearance when preparing for competition and the gains are usually solid and remain after use. However, Stanozolol should not be used on its own during dieting, as it does not protect the bodybuilder from losing muscle, so should ideally be combined with a compound such as Trenbolone and for this stack most bodybuilding take 50mg of Stanozolol every 1 to 2 days, alongside 100mg of Trenbolone every other day.

Other steroids which bodybuilders combine with Stanozolol during competition preparation include; Drostanolone Enanthate, Boldenone Undecylenate, Fluoxymesterone, Oxandrolone, Testosterone Propionate, Methenolone Enanthate, and HGH. Stanozolol is also a favourite with older bodybuilders who make good progress when stacking Stanozolol with Nandrolone Decanoate or Methenolone Enanthate with virtually no side-effects. Also injecting

Stanozolol into certain muscles has become increasingly popular since bodybuilders have noticed that this leads to an accelerated growth of the affected muscle.

DELIVERY

Stanozolol is generally produced in a strength of 50mg per ml, in 1 ml single dose ampoules and 10ml multi-dose vials, as well as 5mg, 10mg and 50mg tablets.

COSTS

Approximate costs of Stanozolol on the black market (in GBP / USD) at the time of writing this booklet (May 2016):

- 50 x 5mg tablets between 20 and 30 GBP / 40 and 60 USD
- 50 x 10mg tablets between 25 and 35 GBP / 50 and 70 USD
- 50 x 25mg tablets between 25 and 35 GBP / 50 and 70 USD
- 50 x 50mg tablets between 50 and 60 GBP / 100 and 120 USD
- 1ml x 50mg single dose ampoule between 5 and 6 GBP / 10 and 12 USD.
- 10ml x 50mg per ml multi-dose vial, between 40 and 50 GBP / 80 and 100 USD

DROSTANOLONE ENANTHATE

Drostanolone Enanthate, more commonly known as Masteron, an injectable steroid almost solely by bodybuilders for conditioning and cutting purposes, such as hardness, dryness and overall definition.

The active life is around 8 days and can be detected in the system for up to 3 months. Its side-effects are minimal but in large doses can be similar to Nandrolone Decanoate. Stacked with Trenbolone and the Testosterones, along with an anti-aromatization compound like Letrozole, male bodybuilders usually take between 400 and 600mg per week, with female bodybuilders taking around 100mg per week.

DELIVERY

Drostanolone is generally produced in a strength of 100mg per ml, in 1 ml single dose ampoules, 10ml and 20ml multi-dose vials.

COSTS

Approximate costs of Drostanolone on the black market (in GBP / USD) at the time of writing this booklet (May 2016):

- 1ml x 100mg single dose ampoule between 5 and 7 GBP / 10 and 14 USD
- 10ml x 100mg per ml multi-dose vial, between 40 and 50 GBP / 80 and 100 USD
- 20ml x 100mg per ml multi-dose vial, between 50 and 60 GBP / 100 and 120 USD

MESTEROLONE

Mesterolone, commonly known as Proviron, is an oral compound similar to Stanozolol and Oxandrolone and is not too liver toxic.

Because of its anti-estrogenic properties bodybuilders use Mesterolone to give a hardened and quality look to muscles and, when taken alongside a testosterone compound, helps prevent estrogen build up which means, if you are taking Mesterolone and a testosterone, you will actually have more testosterone floating around the body and more androgen receptors bound to by the Mesterolone, thus causing more fat loss.

Testosterone and Mesterolone are an ideal stack as both compounds act to enhance the effect of the other. Put simply; Mesterolone is a steroid which can make other steroids more effective. Bodybuilders also use Mesterolone during Post Cycle Therapy for a bridge between cycles it has little effect of the body's own production of testosterone.

Most male bodybuilders take between 100mg to 200mg a day, while female bodybuilders take from between 25mg to 50 mg a day. The active life is around 12 hours so dosages are best split up,. Mesterolone can be detected in the system for up to 6 weeks.

DELIVERY

Mesterolone is generally produced in a strength of 25mg and 50mg tablets.

COSTS

Approximate costs of Mesterolone on the black market (in GBP / USD) at the time of writing this booklet (May 2016):

- 50 x 25mg tablets between 35 and 45 GBP / 70 and 90 USD
- 50 x 50mg tablets between 45 and 55 GBP / 90 and 110 USD

STENBOLONE

Stenbolone, commonly known as Anatrofin, is an injectable steroid, very similar to Methenolone Enanthate, Drostanolone Enanthate and Mesterolone, used by bodybuilders for conditioning, recovery, rejuvenation as well as preservation of muscle tissue during cutting phase. Stenbolone doesn't aromatize so it doesn't cause estrogenic side-effects. It is often quite hard to find and fairly expensive compared to the more common compounds.

It has an active life of around 3 days and dosages taken are usually 100mg to 200mg every day or every other day.

DELIVERY

Stenbolone is generally produced in a strength of 100mg per ml, in 1 ml single dose ampoules only.

COSTS

Approximate costs of Stenbolone on the black market (in GBP / USD) at the time of writing this booklet (May 2016):

- 1ml x 100mg single dose ampoule between 10 and 15 GBP / 20 and 30 USD

SANABOLICUM

Sanabolicum probably the most talked about injectable anabolic steroid on the planet. Bodybuilders use it to achieve almost any goal, whether muscle building or cutting for competition, and Sanabolicum has an outstanding safety record. Sanabolicum does various important things; it promotes nitrogen retention in the muscle cell, increases the body's levels of IGF-1, significantly increase the levels of androgen receptors in muscle, significantly improve recovery by increasing the number of red blood cells, and speeds up the rate of glycogen replenishment after exercise. It is also an excellent fat-loss agent. It does aromatizes slightly, but only at around 20% of the rate of testosterone, so side-effects are minimal.

Most male bodybuilders take between 100mg and 300mg and female bodybuilders between 50mg and 100mg every three days.

It has an active life of about 13.5 days with a detection time up to 18 months. Sanabolicum is formidable when stacked with Testosterone and Dianabol, and substantial muscle size and strength gains can be achieved. It can also be used in a cutting cycle with Testosterone and Stanozolol or Oxandrolone.

DELIVERY

Sanabolicum is generally produced in a strength of 100mg per ml, in 1 ml single dose ampoules and 10ml multi-dose vials.

COSTS

Approximate costs of Sanabolicum on the black market (in GBP / USD) at the time of writing this booklet (May 2016):

- 1ml x 100mg single dose ampoule between 10 and 15 GBP / 20 and 30 USD
- 10ml x 100mg per ml multi dose vials between 80 and 110 GBP / 160 and 220 USD.

HUMAN GROWTH HORMONE

Human Growth Hormone (HGH or GH) is produced in the body by the pituitary gland. It is a protein that stimulates the body cells to increase in size, as well as to facilitate a much more rapid cell division than usual. It also heightens the movement of amino acids through cell membranes and increases the rate at which these cells convert these molecules into proteins which, for bodybuilders, has a significant impact on muscular development. Also, Human Growth Hormone increase the rate at which the cells use fats, so not only does the bodybuilder put on muscle, he/she also significantly loses body-fat.

Most bodybuilders seem to be finding best results from using 0.5iu to 1iu injection every other day over a typical 24 week period, although some are taking a lot more for a lot longer, and many professional bodybuilders stay on Growth Hormone all year, funds permitting. Also, maintaining year-round 6 to 7 bodyfat percentage seems to be normal for male bodybuilders continually taking growth hormone, even when not on steroids.

Most bodybuilders start using HGH once they have reached a peak with steroid use. Using HGH on its own however does not produce as significant results as it would by combining it with IGF1, insulin, testosterone, a thyroid medication such as T3, as well as an Aromatase Inhibitor to stop the conversion of testosterone into estrogen. These stacks and cycles are resulting in massive gains in muscle mass and is what has brought the pharmacology of bodybuilding and muscle building into the 21st Century.

DELIVERY & COSTS

Human Growth Hormone is produced in a strengths measured in International Units and not mg, and comes in a range of different single dose ampoule / multi-dose vial sizes, from 1iu through to 10iu. Prices vary hugely too, depending upon the brand and country of origin, but generally range from between 15 and 25 GBP / 30 and 50 USD per iu.

INSULIN

WARNING - take too much insulin and you will fall into a coma and die. Fact.

Insulin. Bodybuilders use insulin alongside Growth Hormone, IGF1, steroids and testosterone for massive muscle gains. Insulin is one of the most powerful anabolic agents in the world. Insulin is a protein secreted by the pancreas which significantly stimulates muscle protein synthesis beyond what your body could normally convert and, for this reason, bodybuilders using insulin should consume at least 2.5 grams of protein per kilo of bodyweight, but preferably up to 3 to 4 grams of protein per kilo bodyweight. Which means a 220lb (100kg) bodybuilder must ideally consume up between 250 and 400 grams of protein a day.

Insulin can also increase bone density, and increases the body's own Insulin-like Growth Factor (see IGF). It also increases hormones required to stimulate testosterone production. Insulin has anabolic synergy when combined with growth hormone, IGF, anabolic steroids and a fat-burner. to provide the most potent muscle-building and fat-burning cycle possible.

Insulin can easily stimulate body-fat storage, but bodybuilders usually counter this by taking a fat-burner or thyroid (see T3). Bodybuilders use insulin in three ways. Firstly they take a little with each meal, 5 or 6 times a day. The average dose seems to be 1iu to 2iu (international units not mg or mcg!) per injection, although some bodybuilders have been reported to be taking two to three times this amount, starting at a smaller dose and work up over 7 to 10 days. Insulin injections are subcutaneous - below the skin but above the muscle with an insulin needle. Each meal must contain plenty of mixed carbs and least 40g of protein and a tiny amount of essential fats.

The second way bodybuilders take insulin is to take 1iu with a post-workout shake or meal, eventually building up to 1iu per 10 kilo of bodyweight. Most bodybuilders see better gains with this method. However, post-workout meal should contain at least 100 to 200 grams of mixed carbs, 40 to 50 grams of protein and a tiny amount of essential fats.

The third way is the most dangerous, it is to use both methods; 1iu to 2iu with each meal and up to 1iu per 10 kilo of bodyweight with the post workout meal. Blood sugar levels should be monitored very carefully with this method and the onset of any tiredness should be very quickly countered by mixed carbohydrates.

DELIVERY & COSTS

Insulin is produced in a strengths measured in International Units and not mg, and comes in a range of different single dose ampoule / multi-dose vial sizes. Prices vary hugely too, depending upon the brand and country of origin, but generally range from between 5 and 7 GBP / 10 and 14 USD per iu.

SIDE EFFECT REDUCTION AGENTS & POST STEROID THERAPY...

Tamoxifen Citrate more commonly known as Nolvadex is an oral compound used by bodybuilders as side-effect prevention, as well as during Post Cycle Therapy (PCT). Estrogen build-up is a common side-effect for most bodybuilders on most steroids, so Tamoxifen Citrate is used to block estrogen from binding to the receptors which helps prevent many of the side-effects that occur because of this build-up. A daily dose of 10mg per day is the normal dose used. Many bodybuilders also use Tamoxifen Citrate 3 to 4 weeks Post Steroid Therapy, alongside hCG. This is where most bodybuilders will get the most benefit from using Tamoxifen Citrate.

Clomiphene Citrate more commonly known as Clomid is an oral compound used by bodybuilders coming off steroids and beginning Post Steroid Therapy. Clomid stimulates the release of the own body's production of testosterone, as well as a preventative measure against gynecomastia. Bodybuilders can use Clomid safely for up to 4 months, however the usual dose and method is 150mg per day for 10 days, 100mg for another 10 days and then 50mg for the final 10 days, which seems to restore most testosterone levels to normal. There are a very few side effects associated with Clomid use, with some people reporting vision issues with sustained high dosages of 150mcg a day for over a month.

Anastrozole is an oral compound used by bodybuilders to actively block the aromatase enzyme which is responsible for a great many negative side-effects commonly associated with steroid use, such as gynecomastia and excess water retention. Bodybuilders using Anastrozole significantly reduce and often eliminate many side-effects altogether. Although Anastrozole can be used during Post Steroid Therapy, bodybuilders generally use it during a cycle.

For the average steroid user, a dose of 0.5mg every other day will normally be enough, however heavy steroid users may need 1mg every other day. Also, before competition, some bodybuilders use 1mg a day for 7 to 14 days in order to achieve a much harder and dryer look.

Letrozole is an oral compound used as side-effect prevention for bodybuilders on the heaviest bulking or cutting cycles, and those incorporating androgens in their cycles. Letrozole is a must for competitive bodybuilders as no other ancillary compound supports the sought after dry and tight appearance quite as well. Letrozole can also reduce / eliminate / reverse existing gynecomastia if taken for at least 60 days. Most bodybuilders use between 0.25 to 0.5mg a day, however one side-effect of using over 0.25mgs day is a significant reduction in sex-drive. Letrozole is also used by some bodybuilders for their Post Steroid Therapy as it can raise the hormones necessary for the body to produce its own testosterone. Letrozole has a 2 to 4 day half-life which should be taken into consideration when planning a dosages.

Aromastab is an oral compound used as side-effect prevention for bodybuilders. Although very similar compound to Arimidex and Letrozole (above), Aromastab however increases total testosterone production while also increasing natural IGF1 production, which Arimidex and Letrozole cannot do.

HCG (human chorionic gonadotropin) is a naturally occurring peptide hormone, produced by the embryo in the early stages of pregnancy and then by part of the placenta to help control a pregnant woman's hormones. It is used by bodybuilders to restart the body's natural testosterone levels after a long cycle of steroids, and to help prevent testicular atrophy, or restoring testicles back to their original size after testicular atrophy. An average dose of HCG during a steroid cycle is between 500iu to 1000iu (international units) injection every week or two. For

PCT most bodybuilders take between 250iu to 500iu every other day for a 2 to 3 week period, and should always be used with a compound such as Nolvadex. The half-life of HCG is approximately 4 to 5 days. Once opened and mixed, the substance should be stored in a refrigerator.

ABOUT... ROBIN BARRATT

Former nightclub doorman and bodyguard, and now an author and publisher, Robin has written six best-selling true crime books; *Doing the Doors, Confessions of a Doorman, Bouncers and Bodyguards, Respect and Reputation* (with prisoner Charles Bronson), *Mammoth Book of Hard Bastards,* and *Britain's Toughest Women.* He has also written a large number of other books including two travel anthologies about Bahrain, a number of poetry collections as well as the best-selling *101 Fascinating Facts about Anabolic Steroids in Bodybuilding* and *Finding Work as a Close Protection Specialist (Bodyguard).* Robin also compiles, edits and publishes *On The Doors* magazine (OnTheDoors.com) the only lifestyle magazine in the world for those working security in nightclubs, bar and venues across the UK and abroad.

For details of all of Robin's books go to his Amazon author's page:

www.amazon.co.uk/Robin-Barratt/e/B0034PY84C/

You can contact Robin at: RobinBarratt@yahoo.com